THE
COMPETENCIES
POCKETBOOK

By Roger Mills

Drawings by Phil Hailstone

"Clear, concise and thought-provoking. Provides a logical step-by-step guide for deciding why and how to use competencies."
June Isherwood, Head of Support Services, Nirex

Published by:
Management Pocketbooks Ltd
Laurel House, Station Approach,
Alresford, Hants SO24 9JH, U.K.
Tel: +44 (0)1962 735573
Fax: +44 (0)1962 733637
E-mail: sales@pocketbook.co.uk
Website: www.pocketbook.co.uk

This edition published 2004.
Reprinted 2006, 2008.

© Roger Mills 2004.

British Library Cataloguing-in-Publication
Data – A catalogue record for this book is
available from the British Library.

ISBN 978 1 903776 25 4

Design, typesetting and
graphics by **efex ltd**.   Printed in U.K.

CONTENTS

CONTENTS

1 INTRODUCTION

WHY YOU SHOULD READ THIS BOOK

This pocketbook is about competencies: what they are and how to use them profitably for you and your organisation.

You need to read it if:

- You don't know what competencies are but feel you should
- You've heard about competencies and want to know more
- Your organisation plans to use competencies but you are in the dark or anxious
- You want to understand how competencies can help you in your work and career
- Your organisation uses competencies but you're not clear how to use them
- You want to introduce competencies into your organisation and need to know how
- You are launching competencies and want a concise booklet to give out to staff
- Your own competency scheme doesn't work and you need to revive it!
- You see problems in your organisation and think that competencies could help

LISTEN OUT FOR VERBAL CLUES

If, in your organisation, you hear people saying…

'I'm not clear about what's expected from me'

'My manager sets ridiculously high standards compared with the others'

'Yes, we have a company vision and values but they don't really affect me'

'My manager and I saw things differently at my appraisal'

'I can't see a future for me here; I don't feel I fit in'

'My manager criticised me unfairly; gave me really unfair ratings at my appraisal'

'I can't get my manager to talk seriously with me about my development'

'What must I do to get promoted around here?'

…then you might want to read this pocketbook to find out why.

FURTHER INDICATORS

Or, if there are issues such as…

- Can't get the right people
- Can't keep good people – they join but don't stay long
- Managers find appraisals difficult or embarrassing to do
- Training is unfocused or doesn't deliver what's needed
- Managers are inconsistent in the way they treat their people
- People don't buy in to the organisation's vision and values
- People are promoted but don't perform the new job as expected

…then, once again, you might want to read this pocketbook to get some ideas about dealing with them.

WHAT ARE COMPETENCIES?

There has been much debate regarding the differences between competence, competency and competent. The Oxford English Dictionary gives (among others) the definitions:

Competent (adj) – having adequate skill, properly qualified, effective.

Competence (and competency) (n) – power, ability, capacity (*to do, for* a task etc).

However, in the 1970s David McClelland[1] and Richard E. Boyatzis[2] of US management consultants Hay-McBer carried out research that led to a more specific use of the term **competency** that is now widely used in business.

[1, 2] – See Further Reading, page 126

INTRODUCTION

DEFINITION OF (A) *COMPETENCY*

The most common definitions in recent years are:

- An underlying characteristic of an individual that is causally related to criterion-referenced effective and/or superior performance in a job or situation (Spencer[3] 1993)
- A characteristic and measurable pattern of behaviours, knowledge and skill that contributes to superior job performance (Dubois[4] 1993)

Or, more simply put:

A competency describes the behaviour or actions that can be seen when a job is being done well.

[3,4] – See Further Reading, page 126

THE DIFFERENCE BETWEEN KNOWLEDGE, SKILL AND COMPETENCY

Knowledge   Information that has to be learned and is recalled to carry out a job.

Eg, a person can know how to use a particular piece of computer software – but not necessarily be able to do it.

Skill   The application of that knowledge in a practical way to achieve a result.

Eg, continuing the above example, the person may be able to use a keyboard and by doing so apply their knowledge of the software and produce a document.

Competency   The application of that skill in a way that results in work done to a **specified standard**. Most importantly, the competency will be defined so that it includes a number of statements describing **how well** the job must be done.

Eg, the person can use their knowledge and skill of the software to produce a letter in the company format, with no mistakes and within a given time.

NOTES

WHY ORGANISATIONS USE <u>COMPETENCIES</u>

SUMMARY OF BENEFITS

Some of the more cynical types say they use competencies 'because it's the fashionable thing to do' or 'it's the latest Human Resource fad'. However, the more enlightened recognise the benefits that both organisations and their people can gain by having expectations better explained.

Most organisations that use competencies do so to help them:

- Get consistency in what they do across the organisation
- Make sure people are treated equitably
- Communicate with their people
- Improve their stakeholder relationships
- Identify how they can improve
- Establish high standards of quality and performance

TO ACHIEVE CONSISTENCY

Organisations achieve **consistency** and **equity of treatment** by:

- Making sure that any given competency is defined in the same way across the *whole organisation*

- Helping managers to interpret and assess their staff against the same *defined and agreed standards*

- Using competencies to *underpin* their Human Resource *policies and procedures*

- Encouraging their people to develop the *right* competencies for success

WHY ORGANISATIONS USE COMPETENCIES

TO COMMUNICATE EFFECTIVELY

Organisations use competencies when **communicating** with their people by:

- Clarifying their *expectations* and the standards they wish to see
- Defining the *company culture* – 'how we do things around here'
- Explaining and communicating *change*
- Carrying out activities that train, develop and *enable their people to perform well*
- Translating the organisation's values into *everyday actions*

And they *may* use competencies to:

- Get feedback on how the company is performing
- Contribute to performance-related pay/reward systems

WHY ORGANISATIONS USE COMPETENCIES

TO RAISE PERFORMANCE

Organisations use competencies to **improve** standards and **raise company performance** by:

- Identifying, developing and reinforcing the competencies that are delivering *real* business performance

- Implementing competency assessments to *identify strengths and weaknesses*, and so make strategic decisions

- Surveying customers and staff about *organisational performance*, and thereby measuring growth and progress

- Reinforcing the *values* of the organisation

WHO ARE THE USERS?

Users of competencies are widespread and numerous, including those in:

Industry and Manufacturing	Banking and Finance	Local and Regional Government
Education Authorities and Establishments	Charities and other not-for-profit organisations	Large and small organisations (50,000 to 50!)
Central Government Departments	Professional institutions and Societies	Private companies and PLCs

COMPETENCY ORIGINS AND THE FORMATS USED

THE ORIGIN OF COMPETENCIES

Ways of assessing people and their performance go back (some claim) as far as Roman times. Since then more sophisticated ways have been developed, especially by the military (War Office Selection Boards in the 1940s). Assessment centres and development centres have been used ever since for seeking out those people with certain *qualities* or *attributes*.

However, the generally recognised founders of the modern competency movement were David McClelland and Richard E. Boyatzis who worked for US-based management consultants Hay-McBer.

Others have since further developed competencies and they are now a widely used business tool.

THE ORIGIN OF COMPETENCIES

Competencies have broadly developed in two ways:

- Much of the work in the US has concentrated on identifying the competencies displayed by *superior performers* – the purpose being to recognise their competencies and select, train or otherwise develop others to emulate their behaviour

- In the UK, competencies were applied in a major way in the development of *standards* for main occupational groups – the principal outcome of which has been the development of National Vocational Qualifications (NVQs)

This led to differing philosophies depending on which approach was preferred. The UK model focuses on defining a *minimum standard* to be achieved, whilst the US model defines what a superior performer would do. Both are legitimate systems and either may be adopted according to the organisation's objectives.

DIFFERENT TYPES OF COMPETENCY

Depending on its purpose and preferences, an organisation may create a set of competencies (collectively known as a **competency framework**) using a number of different types of competency. Typically it might contain:

Core competencies
Those that support the declared mission and values, and are usually applicable to all jobs in the organisation.

Common competencies
Those other (non-core) competencies with a common definition, for use in *certain jobs* across the whole organisation (eg, influencing, strategic awareness, leadership).

Technical or job-specific competencies
Those that are applicable to a particular group or 'family' of jobs (eg, territory planning, software programming).

Some organisations only use core competencies, others use core and common, and yet others use all three types.

COMPETENCY ORIGINS AND THE FORMATS USED

WHAT COMPETENCIES LOOK LIKE

The format or appearance of a competency will depend on many factors – what type it is, how many competencies there are in the framework, the individual preference of the writer etc.

Some competencies are very simple in their layout and others are quite detailed. The common factors in any competency format are:

- The title or label for the competency (eg, teamwork, customer focus, creativity)
- A number of statements or **behavioural indicators** that explain what the *desired performance or effective behaviour* looks like

And there will usually be:

- A brief definition of what the label means – it may be a generic definition or one created by, and specific to, the organisation

WHAT A SIMPLE COMPETENCY LOOKS LIKE

Title: Teamwork

Definition: This competency concerns the effective and supportive relationships within a team and how the members work together to achieve common goals.

Behavioural indicators (of effective behaviour):

- Establishes and maintains good working relationships; is co-operative and helps when needed
- Actively contributes; gets involved; volunteers
- Respects the effort and time of others; is punctual for meetings
- Shares own knowledge and expertise to help others
- Asks for help from other team members when necessary
- Listens to colleagues and recognizes their knowledge and skill

Is this what competences look like in your organisation? Perhaps they are a bit more detailed…

MORE DETAILED FORMATS

Some organisations will want to expand the amount of information included in the competency. For example:

- **Negative indicators:** these show the sort of behaviour that the organisation does **NOT** want to see (sometimes called *ineffective behaviour*)

- **Outstanding:** these indicators show what **extra** a person would need to be doing to be excellent or outstanding in the competency; it often defines the *role model*

- **Levels:** where a group of jobs requires an increasing degree of a competency as the 'seniority', responsibility or complexity level increases (NB This is not necessarily the same as grade or level within the organisation structure)

Whilst these may make a competency look complicated on first inspection, they are only variations on the simple theme.

25

COMPETENCY ORIGINS AND THE FORMATS USED

EXAMPLE 1

A competency with negative and outstanding indicators may look like this:

Teamwork

Definition: this concerns the effective and supportive relationships within a team and how the members work together to achieve common goals.

Indicators of effective behaviour:

- Establishes and maintains good working relationships; is co-operative and helps when needed
- Actively contributes; gets involved; volunteers
- Respects the effort and time of others; is punctual for meetings
- Shares own knowledge and expertise to help others
- Asks for help from other team members when necessary
- Listens to colleagues and recognizes their knowledge and skill

Continued ▶

COMPETENCY ORIGINS AND THE FORMATS USED

EXAMPLE 1

Indicators of outstanding behaviour:
- Generates enthusiasm, team spirit and opportunities for colleagues to achieve results
- Anticipates the needs of the team and makes arrangements accordingly
- Aware of 'greater' team and builds bridges and partnerships between functions; breaks down barriers
- Will take the lead when necessary; ensures team members pull in same direction

Negative indicators (or indicators of ineffective behaviour):
- Not willing to be accountable; ducks out
- Is insular, loner, not an active player
- Arrogant; looks after own interests
- Disruptive, un-cooperative, unreliable, lets others down
- Hijacks success; allocates blame
- Never volunteers

COMPETENCY ORIGINS AND THE FORMATS USED

EXAMPLE 2

A competency with more than one level might look like this:

Leadership

Definition: this concerns the ability to motivate and inspire others to achieve collective objectives. It includes taking the initiative with colleagues, formulating goals and providing purpose and direction.

Level 1:
- Acts by example, is credible, has the respect of staff
- Is approachable, gives time to staff and keeps them informed
- Resolves issues and disagreements that arise within the group

Level 2 – as above, plus:
- Sets clear goals so that individual effort aligns with the overall aims of the team
- Takes calculated risks for the good of the team
- Style of working enables others to excel and out-perform the standards normally expected

---

EXAMPLE 2

Level 3 – as above, plus:
- Inspirational, conveys a passion and direction that instils pride and feeling of success
- Is able to gain support from wide range of people
- Can deliver bad news and still get good performance

Negative indicators:
- Fails to value the input of others, dismissive of ideas/suggestions
- Has little or no respect from others; makes derogatory remarks about management, company, or colleagues
- Motivates by fear, is inconsistent or over-reacts
- Inconsistent in dealings with group members; has favourites or abuses position of authority

(In this example, the levels are cumulative with Level 1 as the base)

NOTES

DEVELOPING A
COMPETENCY FRAMEWORK

DO *STANDARD* COMPETENCIES EXIST?

Answer: No! Although there are numerous sources of 'ready-made' competencies.

Some commercial organisations make their competencies available to outsiders

Some writers have published what they offer as a definitive list of competencies - sometimes referred to as a competency library

Others, such as professional organisations and government, also publish their competencies

YOUR COMPETENCIES

Or, develop competencies that are specific and unique to your organisation

WHY MOST ORGANISATIONS PREFER TO DESIGN THEIR OWN

Whilst it is tempting to use competencies that are freely available from these ready-made sources, most successful organisations will prefer to develop their own framework and tailor their own competencies because:

- They want to use language that suits their organisation's culture
- Using competencies designed by someone else may lead the organisation in the wrong direction
- Every organisation is different and works in different ways. What suits one may not suit another. Each organisation must identify the *right* competencies for them
- They wish to develop a competitive advantage by developing and using their own unique competencies

They will decide for themselves which ones are important, what detail they will go into, the format to use and the detailed indicators they contain.

DEVELOPING COMPETENCIES

Development of a competency framework should start with a clear understanding of:

- Why the organisation wants a competency framework and how it will be used

- Who is going to manage the project and who else will be involved (a steering group or working party might be appropriate)

- What methodology to use

- How to communicate with everyone, both during the design and the roll-out phases

And *most importantly:*

- How committed the top team are to the project

DEVELOPING COMPETENCIES

There is no hard and fast rule for designing either the framework or the competency definitions and indicators. Whoever is managing the project, whether an individual or a working party/steering group, will need to become conversant with the subject and help guide many of the decisions.

By their very nature, certain types of competency will need to be decided and defined by different people. For example, core competencies must be developed with the intimate involvement of the top team (board of directors, governors, trustees etc).

DEVELOPING COMPETENCIES – HOW?

Several techniques are used to develop the framework and define the competencies. The principal methods favoured by specialists are:

Structured interviews using one or more specialised techniques:

- The *repertory grid interview* is often used to determine what the most significant competencies are

- *Behavioural event interview or critical incident interview* may be used both to determine the critical competencies and then to define the behavioural indicators

Or group methods:

- Focus groups which may be specified (top team, high performers, particular job holders) or a representative sample ('diagonal slice', volunteers or randomly selected)

- Group debate, usually to review outputs and make decisions

Details of each of these can be found in various textbooks or via the internet.

DEVELOPING COMPETENCIES – WHO?

The success or failure of a competency framework often starts at the design stage, or even earlier. To ensure later credibility, as many people as possible should be involved in the process. Whether at the initial design, review or trialling applications, the more people who have an input to the process the better will be the support at implementation.

A typical competency development project will have a number of stages that will allow wide involvement:

- Initial concept and agreement must involve the top team
- A project manager and steering group will involve, say, 6-12 people from across the organisation
- Developing competencies should involve many people, especially if job-specific competencies are to be part of the framework
- Any output from the design process will need to be reviewed and trialled. These further stages give opportunities for even more people to become involved

DEVELOPING COMPETENCIES – WHO?

A typical approach for an organisation might be:

Type of competency	Who is involved	How	Trialling and refining	Roll-out
The framework	Project manager, steering group and top team	Research, taking advice and group discussion	Cross-section of employees	To all employees
Core	Top team members	Structured interviews and group discussion	Cross-section of employees	To all employees
Common	Cross-section of employees	Focus groups	Further cross-section groups	To all employees
Job-specific	Group of high-performing job holders	Interviews and/or focus groups	Other selected job holders	Remaining job holders
Various applications	Project manager, steering group and cross-section of employees	Research, taking advice and group discussion	Further cross-section groups	Remaining job holders

ASSESSING COMPETENCIES

ASSESSING COMPETENCIES

WHY IS ASSESSMENT NECESSARY?

In most of the applications on the later pages, there is a requirement for some form of *assessment* of the individual's competence. This is so that the individual (or their manager, coach, mentor) can identify the gap between the defined (expected) behaviour and what they have actually done or are doing.

Assessment is not always easy.

One of the difficulties of any assessment process is to maintain objectivity. In appraisals, for example, the most frequent source of dissatisfaction is when subjective judgements are required (and disputed).

Good, bad, satisfactory, unsatisfactory, marks out of..., A to E, fair and poor – these are all ratings that appear in many appraisal schemes and rely on a personal interpretation of what is expected.

WHY IS ASSESSMENT NECESSARY?

By using competencies much progress can be made towards defining more clearly exactly what is expected (or *how* the individual should be performing).

By their very nature (ie, defining the behaviours) competencies clearly illustrate in observable* terms what is expected of the individual.

Thus, the assessment becomes a process of comparing the individual's *actual behaviour* with the *behavioural indicators* shown in the appropriate competency.

* Observable includes: by interview, discussion, visible evidence, inspection, observed behaviour and written material.

ASSESSING COMPETENCIES

THE BASIC ASSESSMENT

By comparing the *actual behaviour* with the *behavioural indicators* the assessment amounts to an individual answering the basic question:

- **'Do I consistently demonstrate this competency in my daily work?'**

If not, they are probably **inconsistent** in the way they demonstrate it because:

- They do *only some of the indicators* **all** of the time, or
- They do **all** of the indicators *but only some of the time!*

Either way, they might wish to do something to change! This might mean getting some more specific feedback, concentrating a bit more on *how* they work, or getting some training or development.

THE BASIC ASSESSMENT

Even with clearly defined competencies and behavioural indicators, personal judgement cannot be eliminated entirely.

It is tempting for both the job holder and the manager to use the indicators as a check-list and to check off each one individually and add up the numbers of ticks and crosses.

This is misleading. Going back to the origins of competency design, it is clear that the behavioural indicators are only that – indicators! The list is not exhaustive; it simply shows a range of typical behaviours that a person might do to demonstrate the competency. There are other things they might do as well as or instead of those.

The indicators should be viewed as a guide (not absolute) and as a collection or basket of behaviours typical of that competency.

ASSESSING COMPETENCIES

BEYOND THE BASIC ASSESSMENT

Some assessment schemes go beyond the basic question, especially those that have negative and/or outstanding indicators in the format.

Even so, the assessment is still fundamentally the same. The indicators are used to identify not only how a person compares with the expected indicators but also if they are doing some of the *outstanding* or *negative* behaviours. If they are, their assessment might be swayed up or down accordingly.

Again, the indicators should be seen as guidance and as baskets of typical behaviours, not as a definitive check-list.

People who *exceed* expectations or perform *outstandingly* in certain competencies may be valuable as **role models, coaches** or **mentors** to others in the organisation.

Too much negative behaviour might undermine or negate the good things you have done!

USING COMPETENCIES
FOR PERSONAL BENEFIT

USING COMPETENCIES FOR PERSONAL BENEFIT

COMMON USES

Organisations use competencies in a variety of ways – some are focused on the individual and some are used to support the organisation's corporate Human Resource and general management procedures.

The most common uses that directly benefit *individuals* are:

- Competency profiles in or alongside job descriptions or role profiles to define what is expected of job holders
- To review performance in the appraisal process
- To assess individual training and development needs
- In 360° feedback processes to provide insights into personal performance
- In career development planning
- Professional development – CPD

CLARITY OF A PERSON'S ROLE

Most organisations provide their employees with job descriptions, role profiles or similar documents that explain what is expected of them in terms of responsibilities or duties. What is often left unspecified is the standard to which the role should be performed.

The required standard is often left open to interpretation, and the first time an individual knows there is a difference between their interpretation and their manager's, is *when something goes wrong!*

To help people understand and perform as their organisation expects, issue a competency profile for their job. This will help them to understand exactly how they need to perform to be successful.

CLARITY OF A PERSON'S ROLE

EXAMPLE OF A COMPETENCY PROFILE

Competency profile

Date prepared....................

Job.............................. Job holder.............................

	Level expected
Core competencies	Level 2
Communication	Level 1
Customer focus	Level 2
Teamwork	Level 2
Working safely	

	Level expected
Common competencies (as required)	Level 2
Influencing	Level 1
Cost and financial awareness	

	Level expected
Technical competencies (as required)	Level 3
Data collection and analysis	Level 2
Information security	Level 2
Technical authoring	

(48) The profile then enables cross-reference to the company's competency definitions and levels.

CLARITY OF A PERSON'S ROLE

The competency profile also helps the person's manager to be fair and equitable when he or she is reviewing performance.

Together with the competency definitions, it gives the standard expected and prompts a discussion about how the individual has performed by comparison. It should also help to resolve problems where some managers may be more demanding than others in what they expect from their staff.

Consistent standards and expectations are obtained by using the same competency profile for the same jobs across an organisation.

49

USING COMPETENCIES FOR PERSONAL BENEFIT

PERFORMANCE MANAGEMENT

Competencies assist in the review of performance when integrated into the performance management and appraisal process.

By assessing a person's performance against the required competencies for their job, an organisation can help its people in a number of ways:

- By understanding the competencies required at the outset, they will know what is expected of them and so there should be no surprise concerning standards at appraisal time

- Competencies underpin, support and contribute to job performance. By assessing competencies as well as actual achievements in the job, people can get better feedback and can then perform better in the future

- Difficulties of inconsistency and subjectivity can be reduced by working with clearly defined competencies

- People are assessed on the actions and behaviour that make a real difference in their jobs (not on their manager's pet practices or beliefs; nor on personality)

In the absence of a competency framework, individuals and managers often struggle to identify the exact cause of performance shortcomings. Competencies provide a valuable clue.

USING COMPETENCIES FOR PERSONAL BENEFIT

TRAINING AND DEVELOPMENT NEEDS

Most organisations using competencies will do so to identify individual training and development needs.

In assessing a person's performance against the desired competencies, a *development gap* may be identified in one or more areas. It is then possible to identify what actions the person might take (or what training to undergo) in order to overcome:

- A direct cause of underperformance in their job, or
- An underlying cause of difficulty

Alternatively, it can be used to help the individual to **exceed** the standards expected by identifying:

- What he or she can do to excel in the competency and, potentially, become a *role model*
- What competencies to develop for future roles in the organisation

Typically, these development gaps will form the basis of a *personal development plan*.

USING COMPETENCIES FOR PERSONAL BENEFIT

TRAINING AND DEVELOPMENT NEEDS
A SIMPLE PERSONAL DEVELOPMENT PLAN

Personal Development Plan

Name.......................... Department...................... Dates from/to........................

Needs identified (typically, identified from review of objectives, new objectives agreed, competency review and potential job changes):

1.

2.

3.

4.

Action planned	By when?	Review What was done, what was learned, how is it being applied, what further learning is needed?	
A. Coaching, projects, work shadowing and other on-job development etc: 1. 2. 3.			
B. E-learning, CBT, distance learning and other self-development learning: 1. 2. 3.			
C. Off-job courses, conferences, secondments etc: 1. 2. 3.			
Other actions planned (eg, job moves):			

USING COMPETENCIES FOR PERSONAL BENEFIT

360° FEEDBACK

Some organisations use competencies in a 360° feedback system, to help provide people with insights into their personal performance. This usually involves asking about 6-10 other people in the organisation to complete a confidential questionnaire about the individual, which will:

- Ask specific questions about how they compare with certain statements (compiled from the competency behavioural indicators)
- Seek responses on a scale that typically ranges from 'strongly agree' to 'strongly disagree'
- Focus on performance and behaviour, not on personality
- Use an intermediary to collate responses and give confidential one-to-one feedback

To get the most from this activity people should:

- Recognise that someone else's perception is their reality!
- Avoid just selecting their friends to complete the questionnaires
- Recognise the time and effort their colleagues have put into it
- Respect that others may see things differently to them
- Accept all feedback as valuable
- Decide which behaviour(s) they wish to change as a result

A TYPICAL 360° FEEDBACK MODEL

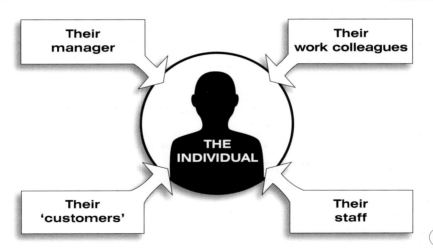

CAREER DEVELOPMENT PLANNING

TAKING STOCK

Competencies can play an important part in the development of career development plans.

To design a career development plan a person would typically start by gaining some insights about their current abilities and interests. They could:

What?	Identify their strengths from past performance appraisals and competency assessments	Recognise their weaknesses from past performance appraisals and competency assessments	Look back over their career, to identify situations and activities that gave them most satisfaction	Use psychometrics such as personality questionnaires, ability tests and aptitude tests	Examine job descriptions and competency profiles
Why?	In order to 'play to them'	In order to improve or avoid them!	In order to replicate them in future	To gain better insight into their abilities and preferences	To seek out career routes that appeal to them

USING COMPETENCIES FOR PERSONAL BENEFIT

CAREER DEVELOPMENT PLANNING

LOOKING FORWARD

The next step for those
working on a career
development
plan is to:

5 Identify roles inside the organisation (or outside, if necessary) that will provide them with the opportunity to practise the skills and competencies and gain the experience.

4 Develop a plan to acquire the knowledge, skills and competencies.

3 Decide what knowledge, skills, competencies* and experience they will need to get from A to B.

2 Define the gap between their current position (A) and the end-point of their plan (B).

1 Identify their long-term goal or end-point of their plan (which may be five years, ten years or whole career!).

*If their employer has a competency framework, the required list of competencies (competency profile) for each job will usually be available either on an in-company intranet or from the Human Resources/Personnel Department

If their employer does not have a competency framework, it is often possible to use one from the many professional bodies and associations that do.

Note: other pocketbooks in the series give more detail on career planning and development.

USING COMPETENCIES FOR PERSONAL BENEFIT

CAREER DEVELOPMENT PLANNING

MAKING THE PLAN

A typical career development planning form might look something like this:

NAME:	YEARS IN PRESENT JOB:	CURRENT POSITION:
DIVISION / DEPARTMENT:		CAREER DIRECTION:
ALTERNATE DIRECTION:		FIVE- OR TEN-YEAR* AIMING POINT: (*Delete as appropriate)

RELEVANT QUALIFICATIONS, ABILITIES AND EXPERIENCE FOR BUILDING CAREER BRIDGES:

DEVELOPMENT NEEDED TO ACHIEVE AIMING POINT:		Roles/positions to gain this:
Knowledge, skills and competencies:	Experience necessary:	

SPECIFIC COURSES, PROJECTS, SECONDMENTS OR ASSIGNMENTS RECOMMENDED:

DATE OF THIS REVIEW:

Example of a Career Development Plan

NAME: J. Flogem	**YEARS IN PRESENT JOB:** Two	**CURRENT POSITION:** Sales administrator
DIVISION / DEPARTMENT: Medical sales	**CAREER DIRECTION:** Senior marketing role	
ALTERNATE DIRECTION: Senior sales role	**TEN-YEAR AIMING POINT:** Senior brand group manager	

RELEVANT QUALIFICATIONS, ABILITIES AND EXPERIENCE FOR BUILDING CAREER BRIDGES:
'communicating', 'influencing' and 'creativity' competencies.
LCCI Cert. in Marketing. High ratings in 'communicating', 'influencing' and 'creativity' competencies.
Experience of medical sales administration, GP and advertising agency liaison.

DEVELOPMENT NEEDED TO ACHIEVE AIMING POINT:

Knowledge, skills and competencies:	Experience necessary:	Roles/positions to gain this:
K: Customer base, sales techniques, product knowledge, market analysis and research, marketing planning, regulatory framework and licensing	Three years selling products into primary care market and key accounts in secondary market	Trainee MR then to medical representative (GP) Key account executive
S: Selling skills, negotiating skills, territory planning, managing agencies	Full marketing responsibility for two - three key brands	Brand manager
C: Negotiating, creativity, strategic perspective, leadership, customer focus, financial awareness	Market planning and new product launch	Senior brand manager

SPECIFIC COURSES, PROJECTS, SECONDMENTS OR ASSIGNMENTS RECOMMENDED:
Courses: In-house sales training programme, product knowledge training, CIM Diploma in Marketing
Projects: Investigate OTC sales potential of ethical product 'x'
Secondment: To a new product launch team during third year in sales

DATE OF THIS REVIEW: June 2004

USING COMPETENCIES FOR PERSONAL BENEFIT

'PROFESSIONAL LADDERS'

In most occupations there is a structure or ladder of increasing complexity or responsibility. This is often reflected in levels of qualification (eg, NVQs) or in grades of membership (eg, graduate, associate, member or fellow). These levels or grades are differentiated in various ways – sequence of examinations, type or length of experience, levels of skills and/or responsibility and, more recently, defined levels of competency.

Examples of 'professional ladders' may be seen on the websites of:

- British Computer Society Industry Structure Model (ISM) at **www1.bcs.org.uk**
- Institution of Civil Engineers at **www.ice.org.uk/rtfpdf/ICE2011RevA.doc** – core objectives
- Health and Beauty Industry Association at **www.habia.org.uk** (shows typical occupational standards/NVQs)

USING COMPETENCIES FOR PERSONAL BENEFIT

CPD

In every line of work there are changes to deal with, new knowledge to gain and new skills to acquire. In most cases these are necessary simply to stay up-to-date. Most professional institutions now require members to undertake a certain amount of continuing professional development (CPD) to retain their membership.

Although it varies slightly from one institution to another, CPD is basically a discipline to ensure that people continually look ahead to the challenges facing them, identify what development they need, plan how they will acquire it and then review their learning afterwards.

As is the case with professional ladders, many institutes, learned societies and similar organisations provide useful information to members and other interested people on the competencies required by their profession. What competencies does yours have?

NOTES

USING COMPETENCIES TO BENEFIT THE ORGANISATION

USING COMPETENCIES TO BENEFIT THE ORGANISATION

HOW?

Organisations often use competencies in their corporate procedures and systems:

- For defining roles
- To identify and analyse training needs
- In succession planning
- To establish, communicate and instil new standards (eg, quality, performance, culture change etc)
- To measure performance and progress through performance scorecard, benchmarking and similar strategic management processes
- For pay and reward – job evaluation, salary review assessments, bonuses etc
- In performance management
- In recruitment and selection using competency-based interviewing and assessment centres design
- In design of learning – including tutored courses, mentoring, coaching and learning resources, e-learning and blended learning

USING COMPETENCIES TO BENEFIT THE ORGANISATION

DEFINING ROLES – COMPETENCY PROFILES

Competency profiles are often used as part of, or alongside, job descriptions or role profiles to define what is expected of job holders.

A competency profile is simply a list of the competencies from the organisation's framework (and, where relevant, the appropriate levels) that apply to that particular job. For simplicity, they usually refer to master competency definitions, rather than describe them fully.

The competency profile then becomes a key part of helping people to understand not only **what** is expected of them but also **how** they should go about doing it.

Individual competency profiles may be developed by specialists, groups or individuals representing the job, or between the job holder and his/her manager, depending upon how many people carry out the same job.

Jobs change and competency frameworks are updated and refined, so competency profiles must be reviewed regularly to ensure they remain current.

USING COMPETENCIES TO BENEFIT THE ORGANISATION

TO IDENTIFY/ANALYSE TRAINING NEEDS

At all levels – individual, department, function and even whole company – competencies are used to identify any gaps that exist between the desirable behaviours and what happens at present.

- At individual level the assessment process (chapter 5) helps to identify an individual employee's training needs, prioritise them and create a personal development plan
- In a department a manager may use individual assessments and then balance strengths and weaknesses across the department to establish where improvement is needed

A simple form of departmental training needs analysis:

	Competencies				Knowledge			Skills	
	Teamwork	Customer focus	Influencing	Attention to detail	Safety awareness	Product knowledge	Statistics	Selling skills	Territory planning
Caroline	✓	✓	✓	✓		✓		✓	✓
Shaquib	✓		✓	✓	✓	✓	✓		✓
Richard		✓	✓			✓		✓	✓
Katie	✓	✓				✓		✓	✓
Mavis	✓	✓	✓	✓	✓			✓	✓

USING COMPETENCIES TO BENEFIT THE ORGANISATION

TO IDENTIFY/ANALYSE TRAINING NEEDS

A similar analysis of individual needs can be done for a specialist *function* (eg, IT, finance, marketing etc).

It is possible to use aggregated individual assessments, but it is also beneficial to use other feedback mechanisms ('customer' surveys, supplier surveys and peer assessments) based on the functional competencies, to decide where the shortcomings are and what needs to be developed.

How to use competencies at *the whole company level* will depend on the size of the organisation and the ease of conducting feedback exercises. Such uses are usually confined to the core (values-driven) competencies (chapter 3) in order to make it manageable and meaningful.

Some of the computer software packages available today will enable the design, online entry and analysis of feedback questionnaires on competencies.

USING COMPETENCIES TO BENEFIT THE ORGANISATION

IN SUCCESSION PLANNING
FOR THE SHORT-TERM

Once upon a time (!) it was common for the best worker (clerk, cashier, scientist, engineer etc) to be promoted to supervisor or manager when a vacancy arose. It was recognised some while ago that this did not necessarily produce good supervisors and managers.

Thankfully the use of succession planning and the quality of appointment decisions have come a long way since then. For some time, succession planning has been a process used to identify probable successors (whether planned replacements or for emergency cover) to existing or future jobs in the organisation. That usually leads to some form of development for those people concerned, to prepare them for a job move.

USING COMPETENCIES TO BENEFIT THE ORGANISATION

IN SUCCESSION PLANNING

FOR THE SHORT-TERM

Using competency frameworks and making competency profiles available and visible for all jobs, enhances the quality of succession planning in a number of ways:

- Individuals can compare their own *strengths* and *weaknesses* with the competency profiles of other jobs, and identify those that may suit them

- Those people making succession plans and appointment decisions are able to use competency profiles to help determine the best candidate

- Assessment or development centres may be arranged to help identify the necessary competencies

And because organisations are changing more frequently, it is often more appropriate for organisations to identify a pool of suitable candidates against a pre-determined set of competencies.

USING COMPETENCIES TO BENEFIT THE ORGANISATION

IN SUCCESSION PLANNING
FOR THE LONG-TERM

Organisations are always striving to make sure there is sufficient high quality talent available, not just for today's needs but also for future challenges. Most will be keen to develop their own in-house talent where possible.

As well as taking into account the track-record, qualifications and *current* abilities of their employees, organisations are more and more trying to foresee the future and identify what kind of people, with what abilities, they will need. Organisations are now trying to single out what the *future competencies* are that people need in order to be successful in facing the challenges ahead.

By establishing what competencies (and specific *behaviour indicators*) are likely to achieve success in the future, organisations seek people from within who demonstrate, or have the ability to develop, those competencies.

You may work in an organisation that has already done this but you may not know! For longer-term development – and especially where high-flyers are concerned – it is still common for some of the decisions about development to be made in private. The more open organisations often use *development centres* to help them find the talented people within. (See also Recruitment and Selection later in this chapter.)

USING COMPETENCIES TO BENEFIT THE ORGANISATION

TO ENHANCE SAFETY STANDARDS

In many industries work and safety standards are regulated and evidence of 'competence' in a job or task is necessary. Many of these standards are regulated by appropriate laws, and people must be regularly assessed to ensure that they are operating according to regulations and procedures.

Once assessed and deemed competent, licences or permits are issued for a finite period of time, after which reassessment is required.

Industries in this group include:

- Railways (maintenance and operations)
- Aerospace (manufacture and maintenance)
- Air travel (operations and maintenance)

TO SUPPORT CHANGE

Business life in the 21st century is as dynamic as ever and getting more so. Almost every organisation is undergoing some kind of **change**. Some common reasons for change are:

WHY ? CHANGE

- To meet stricter regulations
- To become more efficient
- To improve product or service quality
- To respond to customer needs
- To improve sales or profit performance

Unfortunately, the changes frequently fail to make the improvements needed because senior people overlook the fact that, to make the improvements happen individuals have to:

- Understand **why** things must change
- Know **what** they must do differently
- Know **how** to do it
- Be **involved** wherever possible

USING COMPETENCIES TO BENEFIT THE ORGANISATION

TO SUPPORT CHANGE

It is not sufficient to announce a change and then hope that everyone will be positive and help make it work. Much work has to be done to help people understand why the change is necessary, what is expected of them and the role that they must play.

Competencies are invaluable for bringing about change. By defining the different behaviours, as opposed to simply imploring people to act differently, the messages can be explained and reinforced.

Is your organisation changing?

Check-list for change	✔	or	✘
Does everyone know *why* things must change?			
Do they know *how* things need to be different?			
Do people need *to do things differently* in future?			
Does everyone know *what* they must do differently?			
Do they know *how* to do it differently from before?			
Have their *fears* been discussed and resolved?			

TO MEASURE PERFORMANCE

For most organisations it is vital to measure their performance and progress in reaching their goals. Companies try to identify exactly what will make them successful and then monitor these so-called key performance indicators (KPIs) or critical success factors (CSFs) in order to track their progress and make decisions when required.

Almost every organisation uses financial performance to measure itself, and most use other quantifiable measures – sales income, production output, quality performance, new product development etc. But, an increasing number use more sophisticated measures such as a performance scorecard, balanced scorecard[5] and benchmarking, and similar strategic management processes.

Competencies can be measured – *or, at least, people's perception of behaviour can be!*

[5] – See Further Reading, Page 126

USING COMPETENCIES TO BENEFIT THE ORGANISATION

TO MEASURE PERFORMANCE

Ratings of an individual's competencies (see chapter 5) – self, manager and 360° – when collected across an organisation, provide a yardstick. Such subjective internal opinions may be very misleading or self-deluding, and in absolute terms they are not reliable. However, they do provide a starting point from which to monitor and track improvement.

More importantly, similar information gathered from customers, suppliers and other stakeholders through surveys and questionnaires can be very valuable when making strategic decisions.

In the example *whole company* analysis below, actual and target ratings for five core competencies are shown. The improvement targets will help to reinforce and improve future ratings and will point to the priorities for training and development.

Competency	% Rated 'C' or higher		% Rated 'C' (consistent)		% Rated 'E' (exceeding)		% Rated 'O' (outstanding)	
	Actual 2004	**Target 2005**	Actual 2004	**Target 2005**	Actual 2004	**Target 2005**	Actual 2004	**Target 2005**
Stakeholder focus	87	95	53	60	21	20	13	15
Embracing change	56	85	34	65	13	10	9	10
Communicating	68	85	44	55	16	20	8	10
Innovation	72	75	38	40	22	25	12	10
Strategic awareness	69	75	39	45	19	20	11	10

USING COMPETENCIES TO BENEFIT THE ORGANISATION

IN JOB EVALUATION, PAY AND REWARD

Some organisations integrate competencies fully into their reward schemes. This can be by:

- Using levels of competencies in evaluating jobs in a formal job evaluation scheme. When used in this way it is usually in combination with other factors
- Assessing competencies as part of the salary review, once again in combination with other factors such as objective achievement
- Using competencies in incentive pay/bonus schemes, to reward a particular type of behaviour

When planning to use competencies in pay schemes, consider:

- How does the matter of pay affect the integrity of assessments?
- Will individuals be frank about their self-assessment if their income is affected?
- Will managers over-rate someone simply to give a bigger pay rise?
- How can development needs be identified or an organisation's performance be measured when competencies are used in pay?
- What weighting should be given to competencies as opposed to other factors, such as objective achievement?

USING COMPETENCIES TO BENEFIT THE ORGANISATION

IN PERFORMANCE MANAGEMENT

The relationship between objectives and competencies is often a source of debate in organisations. Typically people ask:

- 'Which is more important – achieving my objectives or performing well in the competencies?', or

- 'What should I concentrate on – achieving my objectives or performing well in my competencies?'

Well, of course the short answer is both! But with more careful thought it is clear that competencies are **enablers** that, when performed well, will lead to objective achievement.

Therefore, performing well in the competencies of the job should naturally lead to achieving the objectives *(provided that other factors such as motivation and opportunity are present)*.

IN RECRUITMENT AND SELECTION

RECRUITMENT ADVERTISING

One of the most frequently used applications of competencies is in the area of recruitment and selection. After all, if a company uses competencies it will want to employ people who can perform in that way.

The first step is to make clear in any job advertisements and information sent to applicants that there are certain competencies required for the job (and to work in the company) as well as specific knowledge, skills and experience.

Making it clear to applicants will help to ensure that only those who closely match the requirements apply. This will never entirely filter out unsuitable applicants, but this element of 'self-selection' avoids much wasted time and effort.

PROOF READER REQUIRED

USING COMPETENCIES TO BENEFIT THE ORGANISATION

IN RECRUITMENT AND SELECTION

COMPETENCY-BASED INTERVIEWING

Competency-based interviewing (CBI) differs from conventional interviewing in that questions are asked that allow candidates to demonstrate their experience and past behaviour in respect of a particular competency. Variations include:

- Sending candidates details of the competencies that the company is seeking and, sometimes, even sending the company's own competency details

- Asking candidates to send in or bring to interview specific written examples of their past experiences in a particular competency

- Using probing questions at the interview to establish exactly what the person did at the time and why. This also enables the candidate to fully demonstrate their ability

- Assessing the candidates against the key competencies required

USING COMPETENCIES TO BENEFIT THE ORGANISATION

IN RECRUITMENT AND SELECTION

COMPETENCY-BASED INTERVIEWING

Typical interview questioning:

- 'Tell me about a time when you had to communicate some information to many people.'
- 'What were the factors you considered?'
- 'Why did you choose that method?'
- 'What was the result?'
- 'What would you do differently another time?'

- 'Who do you consider to be your 'customers'?'
- 'How do you know how well you are meeting their needs?'
- 'When was the last time you acted on their feedback?'

- 'How did you ....?'
- 'What was the effect of ....?'
- 'What exactly did *you* do?'
- 'When was the last time you ....?'
- 'Why did you ....?'

USING COMPETENCIES TO BENEFIT THE ORGANISATION

IN RECRUITMENT AND SELECTION

ASSESSMENT CENTRES

Many organisations use assessment centres to select candidates. This often applies to internal candidates as well as to external applicants. An assessment centre will have a number of activities, each one designed to expose a candidate's ability in one or more competency.

A simple matrix for assessment centre design might look like this:

Activity	Communicating	Influencing	Teamworking	Analytical thinking
Presentation	✗	✗		
Group exercise		✗	✗	
Interview	✗			✗
Psychometrics				✗

USING COMPETENCIES TO BENEFIT THE ORGANISATION

DESIGNING LEARNING

Since the most frequent use of competencies is in identifying learning and development needs, it is in the design of learning activities that competencies come into their own.

- Tutor-led programmes can be designed to deliver particular competencies and to particular levels

- Individuals who excel at particular competencies can be developed as coaches and mentors in those competencies

- Learning resources can be acquired or developed for learning specific competencies

- Individual projects can be designed to expose the learner to certain situations, in order to develop particular competencies

To enable the most appropriate learning activities to be selected, ensure there are clear links between each competency and each learning activity. Courses and learning materials should, therefore, show the competency and level that they are intended to develop, and competencies should be linked to a range of learning activities that develop the competency. Company intranets are ideal for communicating this.

WHY SOME COMPETENCY INITIATIVES DON'T WORK

WHY SOME COMPETENCY INITIATIVES DON'T WORK

THEY DON'T DIE, THEY JUST FADE AWAY!

It's usually obvious at an early stage when a competency initiative is not working. There is plenty of vocal opposition, and people find numerous reasons to avoid using it, misunderstand it, misuse it, carry on in the same old way or, even, try to sabotage its launch!

However, most of the competency frameworks that fail don't go down in a blaze of glory! Like many business systems they gradually become out-of-date or unfashionable. They don't usually fail completely; they just fall into disuse and fade away.

To keep competency frameworks effective and valuable to the organisation, work has to be done to keep them fresh, relevant and worthwhile to the people who should be using them.

WHY SOME COMPETENCY INITIATIVES DON'T WORK

COMPETENCY HEALTH CHECK

To establish whether your competency framework is alive and healthy try answering these questions:

Signs of a healthy competency framework	✔ or ✘	
Has your competency framework been reviewed/revised in last 2-3 years?		
Do people talk about the competencies needed for their jobs?		
Do managers review people's performance using the competencies?		
Do competencies permeate other HR systems?		
Does your HR information system record competency information and is it used?		
Are competencies an important part of your succession and development planning?		
For those with intranet, do people access the competency pages frequently?		
Does senior management outside of HR recognise and use the competencies?		
Do competencies figure in any important business decisions?		
Are your training activities aligned with and deliver specific competencies?		
Are there rewards for using the competency framework?		
Do managers use competencies to coach and develop their staff?		

WHY SOME COMPETENCY INITIATIVES DON'T WORK

COMPETENCY HEALTH CHECK

If you can answer 'yes' to most of the questions then it's likely that your competencies are in a healthy state and providing a valuable business benefit to your organisation.

If you answered 'no' to most of the questions then your competencies are unlikely to be of any value – indeed, they may be counter-productive by using valuable management time or *even developing people in the wrong things!*

To be somewhere in-between is quite common. Maybe some of the questions aren't really relevant to your organisation. Perhaps yours is one of the (very rare) companies that doesn't change very much.

However, it probably means that the competencies are not delivering all the benefits they should to the business and they need an overhaul and re-launch.

In the remainder of this section and in the next, we explore the reasons why and what you can do about it.

WHY SOME COMPETENCY INITIATIVES DON'T WORK

INTRODUCED FOR WRONG REASON

Sometimes there are no real business reasons that drive the development of a competency framework. Why was one created in your organisation? Was it developed because:

- Competencies were hailed as the latest HR management tool? **(latest 'fad')**
- The HR department thought they were a good idea? **(HR 'flavour of the month')**
- Your competitors (or any other similar company) had them? **('keeping up with The Jones's')**
- Or for any of the various other cynical reasons?

There must be a *very good business reason* to undertake the work involved to develop an effective competency framework.

FRAMEWORK POORLY DESIGNED

With regard to the various types of competencies discussed earlier, it is sometimes faulty framework design that makes a framework unworkable or *user-unfriendly*. **Is yours:**

- **Too complex?** People will switch off if faced with copious paperwork, especially when it's an untried, untested system or it takes too long to master the processes. Over-complicated behavioural indicators or too many competencies to deal with will be an immediate turn-off.

- **Too simple?** Conversely, if the competencies are too simply written they may not describe the behaviours in sufficient detail to be valuable. If they are too simplistic then the brighter people may feel offended.

- **Too remote?** People will not use the competencies if they don't see the relevance to their everyday work. There needs to be a clear reason for a competency being applied to the individual's job.

FRAMEWORK POORLY DESIGNED (Cont'd)

- **Copied or modified from another company's?** There are likely to be difficulties of ownership. People may not feel they are relevant to their company or to them.
- **Using the wrong competencies?** Using inappropriate or incorrectly defined competencies will point people in the wrong direction. They will probably see the clash between their daily work and the competencies (in which case they will ignore them) or, worse still, the HR and training and management systems may all be developing and rewarding the wrong things!
- **An unsuitable style?** The competencies may use a language that is not suitable to your organisation – too complicated, too verbose or too simple. A complex framework, with very detailed core, common and technical competencies for every job, may be unsuitable where just a simple core competencies framework would be more effective.

FRAMEWORK BADLY INTRODUCED

Sometimes a competency framework fails because insufficient consideration is given to its introduction. Individuals may not understand or, worse, become cynical about it because:

- There is not enough briefing to get understanding of its purpose
- Insufficient training is given to individuals and/or their managers in how to use it
- It is 'parachuted in' without involving or consulting key managers or other users
- There are no benefits perceived by users – 'what's in it for me?'
- It is not seen to be important by management
- It's not supported by management – they don't 'practise what they preach'
- Cynics are not tackled; too many negatives seen
- It's not integrated into other management or people systems in the organisation

THE TIME IS WRONG

Sometimes a very good competency framework can fall flat because it is introduced at the wrong time. Although it is valuable to use competencies to help bring about change, care must be taken to gauge the right time to introduce them.

- When there are many major changes or other initiatives happening in the organisation that are affecting most people, then introduction of competencies is likely to be seen as less important
- If people are unusually busy – new products, new markets, new methods being introduced – then the risk is that competencies will be seen as another chore
- Introducing them during difficult times (eg during downsizing) may be seen as a cynical move by management

ORGANISATION CULTURE UNSUITABLE

Much is talked about the culture of organisations. In a culture of negativity, management control, suspicion or lack of trust between management and employees, introducing competencies may be inappropriate. In such situations it would be seen as:

- Threatening
- Bureaucratic
- A cynical management imposition of tougher standards
- A way of cloning people – taking away their individualism

WHY SOME COMPETENCY INITIATIVES DON'T WORK

COMPETENCIES USED WRONGLY

Sometimes individuals or their managers will misuse the competencies – usually through lack of proper training, but sometimes for questionable or cynical reasons. Some errors are:

- Using the indicators as a rigid check-list against which to mark an individual. The behavioural indicators are just that: *indicators*. Performance of the competency may manifest itself in several different ways that are not necessarily included in the indicators

- Using under-performance as a disciplinary issue. Whilst major under-performance will need attention, the general purpose of a competency framework is for clarification and development

Errors continued over…

COMPETENCIES USED WRONGLY (Cont'd)

- Too much focus on the negatives or under-performance. As with other forms of assessment there must be a balance, and good performance of competencies also needs to be recognised

- Replacing company agreed behavioural indicators with a manager's own personal interpretation. This will lead to inconsistency and unfairness

- Confusion over 'levels'. Whatever level of complexity/seniority/responsibility is required for a job, it is not the same as the rating of the individual against it. For example, a junior supervisor may be expected to perform at, say, Level 1 in leadership and be rated as *outstanding* at Level 1. Yet, a senior management position that requires Level 3 leadership may be held by a person who is rated as *inconsistent* at Level 3

HOW TO MAKE SURE YOUR COMPETENCIES WORK!

HOW TO MAKE SURE YOUR COMPETENCIES WORK!

ESTABLISH A GOOD BUSINESS REASON

In order to be credible and accepted it is vital to understand why a competency framework is being introduced. The more you can show genuine business reasons, the easier it will be to gain commitment from everyone. Chapter two explains in detail most of the reasons why organisations use competencies.

Some good examples are shown in the following case histories:

Case history 1

Creating a common culture

Two major companies merged and the management needed to create an organisation that was different from both of the original companies. They set about defining the vision and values of the new organisation and wanted to communicate how everyone in the organisation could contribute and support the values.

A competency framework was introduced with core competencies describing the behaviours that would support the values. In addition, many of their personnel policies and practices were changed to reflect these new values.

HOW TO MAKE SURE YOUR COMPETENCIES WORK!

ESTABLISH A GOOD BUSINESS REASON

Case history 2

Consistency of treatment

A national charity with a strong religious faith was expanding rapidly and was acquiring and integrating organisations with staff of other faiths.

It was becoming difficult (and potentially illegal) to use religious beliefs as discriminating factors within its personnel practices.

Upon the recommendation of their legal advisers they developed competencies that described the behaviours expected of all staff, irrespective of their particular faith.

HOW TO MAKE SURE YOUR COMPETENCIES WORK!

ESTABLISH A GOOD BUSINESS REASON

Case history 3

Building a positive image

Having received highly critical feedback of arrogance and secrecy, a research organisation wanted to work with all the interested parties, including the public, and restore the reputation of its staff.

First an assessment was undertaken to establish the *lessons learned*. Work was then conducted with all staff to define the organisation's values and identify what had to change in the way they worked.

Descriptions were developed of the behaviour necessary to underpin the values and make clear to everyone how they needed to work in future to demonstrate the organisation's accountability and responsibility to all stakeholders.

These behaviour descriptors were used in recruitment, training and development, and also in the pay and reward system to reinforce their importance.

HOW TO MAKE SURE YOUR COMPETENCIES WORK!

INVOLVE AS MANY PEOPLE AS POSSIBLE AT ALL STAGES

The more people who are involved and contribute to the development of your competency framework, the more chance of overall acceptance and commitment to success you will get. Depending upon the size of the organisation, it may be possible to involve everyone at some stage before finalising the framework, the contents of it and the applications you plan to use.

- Top management, ideally your board of directors, must support the project and be sponsors of the work: hearing proposals, making informed decisions where appropriate and participating in the roll-out

- Forming a cross-company project team to steer the project and become champions of the project will spread participation and increase credibility of the results. Such a team may have HR/personnel or training people on it, but other functions/departments should be well represented. Selecting respected, influential and, sometimes, even non-conformist individuals may help to gain commitment

HOW TO MAKE SURE YOUR COMPETENCIES WORK!

INVOLVE AS MANY PEOPLE AS POSSIBLE AT ALL STAGES (Cont'd)

- Using a cross-section of all employees is an ideal way to help trial and test out your work at various stages of the project. Don't just rely on the same small group of regulars. Get various groups to try out and feed back their experiences of reviewing and using the materials you create

- When developing technical competencies it is essential that they are developed with the involvement of **job holders**. Even if their managers have the final decision on content, it is important that the competencies substantially reflect what the job holders say and do. This is a further opportunity to spread the participation

HOW TO MAKE SURE YOUR COMPETENCIES WORK!

BALANCE PRECISION AND OWNERSHIP

It is tempting to use experts and try to get a well-crafted and precise set of words. However, to get acceptance and ownership by the maximum number of people, you need to have their involvement and to incorporate their views into your framework.

Failure to listen to them, or omitting their suggestions, will only alienate them and defeat the object of their participation.

For a competency framework to be successful there has to be a sensible balance between *perfection and precision* and *acceptance and ownership*.

HOW TO MAKE SURE YOUR COMPETENCIES WORK!

BENEFIT EVERYONE – YOU TOO!

To be really successful any new system must provide a benefit to everyone who is expected to use it – **the 'What's in it for me?' factor**. If people don't recognise how they will benefit from using competencies, then why should they bother to use them? Some of the benefits that everyone can experience are:

- Helps them to understand what is expected of them in their job and 'how to get on around here'

- Leads them to think more clearly about the training and development they want or need

- Enables them to see what competencies other jobs in the organisation need, so they can plan and develop their career towards them

- Helps to make sure they are treated fairly and equitably at appraisal time

- Assists with the development of their 'market worth'

HOW TO MAKE SURE YOUR COMPETENCIES WORK!

GET TOP MANAGEMENT SUPPORT: *DO'S*

No system that is fundamental to the way people work will succeed unless it has full backing from top management.

Top managers show that commitment by:

✔ Interrogating and approving the business case for developing a competency framework

✔ Being sponsors or champions of the competency project

✔ Devoting sufficient time and enthusiasm to their participation at various stages

✔ Encouraging their staff to be involved in the project; nominating their best people for key roles

✔ Being *actively* involved in communicating and supporting the project

✔ Seeking reports and feedback on the project's progress

HOW TO MAKE SURE YOUR COMPETENCIES WORK!

GET TOP MANAGEMENT SUPPORT: *DON'T'S*

Managers can destroy or defeat a good competency framework if they:

✗ Deny or contradict, in private to their own people, the top teams' support

✗ Undermine or disown the project

✗ Fail to release good staff for the project

✗ Implement it half-heartedly in their own departments (or fail to do it at all!)

✗ Fail to practise what they preach! (don't behave appropriately)

HOW TO MAKE SURE YOUR COMPETENCIES WORK!

PROVIDE AMPLE TRAINING AT LAUNCH

Whether you call it *briefing* or *training*, don't underestimate the amount of communicating that must be done. *Giving people a copy of this pocketbook will help*, but it is no substitute for good face-to-face training. Include at least these main items:

- Why you are introducing competencies
- Why it's important to them
- How they will benefit from competencies
- How the system will work in your organisation – process/procedures
- Some practical work about using the competencies (role plays, case studies etc)
- An opportunity to discuss and challenge the competencies
- Some principles of fair assessment
- The evolving nature of the project (will get feedback and modify as appropriate)
- And make it fun!

'Communicate, communicate and communicate, and when you think you've done enough communicating, communicate some more!'

For managers you may also need to run special training in assessment and appraisal skills using competencies.

FIRST PILOT THE PROJECT

People will need to have a chance to talk about and try out the competencies in a relatively safe situation before using them for real. This is especially true if your framework is to be used in performance appraisal and/or if it will affect pay.

When you roll-out the framework, give people a chance at self-assessment in a 'dry run'. This will undoubtedly be self-assessment but may also include an element of manager assessment. This enables people to experience using competencies without significant repercussions, will stimulate questions and will allow managers to discuss future implementation with their staff.

It will act as a full-scale pilot, allowing you to get feedback and make modifications to improve it before it is used. It will also enable any inconsistencies of drafting, interpretation, application of competencies or rating to be identified and corrective action taken.

HOW TO MAKE SURE YOUR COMPETENCIES WORK!

START WITH 'GENTLE' APPLICATIONS

Going straight in to applications that might be seen as high risk, stressful or, even, threatening may be problematic. It is better to start with some non-threatening applications.

High risk

Performance (pay-related)
Job evaluation
Performance scorecards

Medium risk

Customer and supplier surveys
Performance (non-pay)
Career development succession planning

Low risk

360° feedback
Self-assessment
Gap analysis
Training needs identification
Recruitment and selection

(NB: Not all organisations use competencies for all these applications.)

INTEGRATE COMPETENCIES INTO ALL HR/PERSONNEL PRACTICES

Once a competency framework has been established it should be used as the basis for all your people practices (one exception may be the pay and reward system). By doing that you will:

- Ensure consistency of message
- Have a constant reinforcement of the competencies
- Embed them into your business quicker
- Develop a clearer understanding of the relationship between HR/personnel practices

COMPETENCIES ARE
IMPORTANT TO EVERYONE

COMPETENCIES ARE IMPORTANT TO EVERYONE

BETTER JOB PERFORMANCE

The simplest way of using competencies is for a person to assess themselves against the competencies needed by their present job.

By assessing themselves they will be able to recognise parts of their job where they might want to improve. That doesn't imply that they are not doing well; it might be that they want to excel.

It is also likely that their manager will do this and help them to recognise their strengths and development needs.

COMPETENCIES ARE IMPORTANT TO EVERYONE

'GETTING ON' WITHIN THE ORGANISATION

Competencies (particularly the ones we call core competencies) are created to tell people what is expected of them when they work for their particular organisation. It therefore follows that, if they want to develop their career there, they would do well to recognise and develop those competencies.

From this they can see that to 'get on' in the organisation, it is important to recognise what competencies are considered important and to set about developing those.

By defining these core competencies*, an organisation is stating very clearly what the particular things are that it values in its people.

* Different organisations may use different terminology for these

GAINING RESPONSIBILITY/PROMOTION

In their present jobs people will have established what competencies they need and, probably, at what level. If they wish to take on more responsibility it may mean that they need to develop the competencies they have to a higher level. They may also need to acquire other competencies.

By looking ahead at what will be needed for this extra responsibility, they can recognise the gaps they need to fill and the training and development they will need in order to get there. They can then look for opportunities to get this training so that, when the opportunity comes along, they are ready for it.

SHOWING INTEREST IN PERSONAL GROWTH

Organisations generally like to see that employees are interested in improving themselves. That might be in their present organisation or some other one to which they may apply.

By identifying their particular competencies and showing their efforts to improve them, they will be demonstrating that they are not just willing but are able to identify and develop their competencies. 'The ability to recognise and act on your weaknesses is good to have.'

COMPETENCIES ARE IMPORTANT TO EVERYONE

CAREER PLANNING

It is sometimes difficult for a person to recognise career paths that he or she might want to follow. Some people are clear on a career that they want and set about climbing their chosen career ladder. Others might find that knowing the competencies required by certain possible careers will help them to plan.

In their organisation it may be easy to find out what competencies are needed for particular jobs and what levels of the competencies are required. If so, then they can identify and assess themselves against them and develop a career plan.

COMPETENCIES ARE IMPORTANT TO EVERYONE

BECOMING MORE 'MARKETABLE'

Whether or not someone professes to be ambitious, everyone needs to maintain a level of 'marketability'. Gone are the days of assured permanent employment – the so-called 'job for life'. Everyone needs to make sure that they are at least maintaining or developing their market worth.

At any time they may need to seek a new role. That could be for:

A new challenge   Change of present role

Career advancement   More interesting work   Better prospects

More pay   Current job redundant

That may be inside their present organisation or it might be outside it. In either case they will need to make sure they are in the best possible position to secure that job.

Recognising and developing the competencies required by their desired role will help them to develop the necessary competencies and present themselves as the best candidate when the time comes.

NOTES

USING COMPETENCIES TO IMPROVE YOURSELF!

MAINTAINING YOUR 'MARKETABILITY'
EXTERNALLY

Even if you are content with your job and your employer, it is critical that you maintain your 'marketability'. When it comes to people decisions in organisations – whether that is expansion, contraction, organisation structure change or promotions – the decision-makers will look for people who are up-to-date, flexible and prepared to learn and develop themselves. This applies as much to internal decisions as it does to bringing in new people from outside the organisation.

Other pocketbooks address this area in more detail but it is critical for you to maintain and develop your own competencies. Many organisations use competency frameworks and, whilst each will have a slightly different set of behaviours they expect to see in future staff, there is nevertheless a certain commonality between them, especially in the core competencies.

MAINTAINING YOUR 'MARKETABILITY'
EXTERNALLY

Typically, organisations like to look for people who are good at:

- Teamwork
- Communicating
- Managing relationships
- Customer focus

Those are critical to most organisations. Depending on the type of organisation, many also like to see such things as:

- Achievement orientation
- Improvement focus
- Innovation/creativity
- Leadership (for managerial positions)
- Concern for quality

To make yourself more marketable it is important to be capable, not only in the 'technical' aspects or technical competencies of a job, but also in these core competencies. You will need to demonstrate to a potential employer how you do these, either through activities they may ask you to do or by explaining past actions you have taken.

USING COMPETENCIES TO IMPROVE *YOURSELF!*

MAINTAINING YOUR 'MARKETABILITY'
EXTERNALLY

Whatever your particular expertise or skill, you will also be expected to demonstrate your capabilities in the key core competencies. Some organisations will tell you what they are looking for, but even if they don't you can assume that most will look for things beyond the skills of the job. Improve your chances of success by making sure you:

- Look carefully at any recruitment advertising and literature you are sent, to see:
  - If they explain their organisation's values and/or core competencies (they might not use those words exactly in that way)
  - What you can deduce about the company; what it does, how it does it and what its values and core competencies might be
- Design your CV to show the competencies you possess, emphasising those that match what they may be looking for
- Take with you any documents or other evidence that shows your experience and abilities in these areas
- Prepare to talk about what you did in these areas of competence and how you did it
- Talk about what *you* did (not 'we', your colleagues or your manager)

(120)
Similarly, identify the technical competencies needed for the job.

USING COMPETENCIES TO IMPROVE *YOURSELF!*

MAINTAINING YOUR 'MARKETABILITY'

INTERNALLY

The principles that apply to self-marketing in your current organisation are exactly the same as those that apply to external job seeking. If your organisation has a competency framework it is highly likely that you will have had some form of competency assessment. It may also use competency-based interviewing or assessment/ development centres to select for vacancies.

Whatever your company uses (or even if it doesn't have a competency framework) you will still need to make yourself more interesting to those making appointments to jobs. This means ensuring that you maintain and develop the competencies that are considered important.

● Look carefully at any competency frameworks that are used in your organisation

● Find out what competencies and what levels (if applicable) are required for more senior positions

● If your organisation doesn't use competencies, look externally at other organisations, professional institutes or associations that do, to find out what competencies they use for similar jobs

ADVANCING YOUR CAREER

Competencies are extremely valuable in moving your career forward. Often, people are unsure what to learn/improve to help progress, and advice isn't always available. Looking at the competencies that prospective jobs require, will help you decide which ones to develop. A typical approach:

- Use assessments of your competencies – whether done by your manager, by colleagues (360° feedback) or by yourself – to establish your strengths, weaknesses and future preferences
- Work out a development plan that will help overcome your weaknesses (if important to progress your career)
- Identify a reasonable long-term goal – 1-2 years ahead or, even, 5-10 years
- Find out the competencies needed by **that sort of job at that level** from: your own company's framework; a published competency list, eg by web search; a professional institution/association; friends/colleagues in other organisations; and from professional career advice
- Develop a plan to learn/practise the competencies needed. This may involve internal job moves or, even, changing employer

USING COMPETENCIES TO IMPROVE *YOURSELF!*

GETTING THE DEVELOPMENT YOU WANT

Sometimes it may be difficult to get your organisation to provide development opportunities. This may be for a number of reasons, some of which you may be able to do something about.

Why you can't get the development	How to get development
Your organisation doesn't provide any development	• Prepare a *business* case to show how developing your competencies will benefit the company; how you will do even better at your job afterwards • Find ways to develop your competencies outside the organisation: joining clubs, sports officiating, further education or volunteering
Your manager doesn't believe in development	• Demonstrate the benefit to him/her of you being able to do more: take some of their load, become more flexible, become competent in more areas • Do some development activity and (cautiously) let him/her know how your greater skill or knowledge came about
No money available	• Look for ways to develop your competencies that don't cost money: on-job coaching, undertaking special projects, work shadowing, networking, reading, secondments or mentoring

WHAT IF YOUR ORGANISATION DOESN'T USE COMPETENCIES?

Even if your organisation doesn't formally use competencies you can still use them to improve yourself.

- Your organisation may be using something very similar and calling them by a different name, eg standards or behaviours. If so, look to use these in the same way as competencies

- Look at what other companies have got. Find a successful company in the same or similar industry and find out if they use competencies. Many large organisations post their competencies on their websites. Ask friends about what their companies do

- Similarly, you can frequently find a competency framework used by professional organisations, showing competencies that are required for membership

- Wherever you get a competency list or framework from, be sure to look at its relevance to your organisation, your job and your career ambitions. Look particularly at those competencies that are likely to be universally applicable

- Go through the same process as you would when using an in-company scheme, to identify the areas you want to develop

SOME USEFUL WEBSITES FOR COMPETENCIES

At the time of writing, the following websites offer some interesting browsing on, or connected with, competencies.

- For a wealth of occupations with detailed analysis of the skills needed, go to **http://online.onetcenter.org/** This is a US site of the Occupational Information Network

- The competency framework for the UK Senior Civil Service is to be found at **www.cabinet-office.gov.uk/civilservice/scs/competences.htm** This shows a clear and fairly simple set of competencies showing indicators for effective behaviour and ineffective behaviour

- To see the competencies required by graduates joining American Express, go to **www10.americanexpress.com/sif/cda/page/0,1641,17103,00.asp**

- Hints for interviewees attending competency-based interviews are given at **http://legal.monster.co.uk/articles/competency**

- The site of the US organisation 'Management Sciences for Health' contains a Self-Assessment Inventory based on their Supervisory Competencies. A downloadable .PDF version is available for personal use at **http://erc.msh.org/mainpage.cfm?file=96.70.htm&module=toolkit&language= English**

FURTHER READING

1   McClelland, D.C. (1973), *Testing for competence rather than intelligence*. American
    Psychologist, 28, 1-14

2   Boyatzis, R.E. (1982), *The Competent Manager*: A Model for Effective Performance.
    New York: John Wiley & Sons, Inc.

3   Spencer, L.M. & Spencer, S.M. (1993), *Competence at Work: Models for Superior
    Performance*. New York: John Wiley & Sons, Inc.

4   Dubois, D.D. (1993), *Competency-based Performance Improvement: A Strategy for
    Organisational Change*. Human Resource Development Press

5   Kaplan, R.S. & Norton, D.P. (1996), *The Balanced Scorecard*. Harvard Business
    School Press

About the Author

Roger Mills
Roger began his career in science, electronics and engineering but very soon became involved in training and development, starting with skills analysis and training design. Since then he has worked in Strategic HR Development in multi-site UK and global organisations in a variety of industries. Working with people at all levels he has developed and implemented business-driven HR and HRD strategies across functional, industry and geographic boundaries. Over the last 10 years he has designed, developed, implemented and revived competency
programmes in a wide range of companies both as the "insider" and as an external consultant. In 1999 he set up his own consultancy since he "preferred doing what he enjoyed in many companies than doing a routine, repetitive job in one".

Contact
He can be contacted at Glencote Consulting Ltd, 7 Raven Close, Aylesbury, Bucks, HP19 0UP or via his web site at www.glencote.com (or by telephone on 01296 336705 or email at info@glencote.com)

ORDER FORM

Your details

Name _____

Position _____

Company _____

Address _____

_____

_____

Telephone _____

Fax _____

E-mail _____

VAT No. (EC companies) _____

Your Order Ref _____

Please send me:

	No. copies
The _Competencies_ Pocketbook	☐
The _____ Pocketbook	☐
The _____ Pocketbook	☐
The _____ Pocketbook	☐

Order by Post
MANAGEMENT POCKETBOOKS LTD
LAUREL HOUSE, STATION APPROACH,
ALRESFORD, HAMPSHIRE SO24 9JH UK

Order by Phone, Fax or Internet
Telephone: +44 (0)1962 735573
Facsimile: +44 (0)1962 733637
E-mail: sales@pocketbook.co.uk
Web: www.pocketbook.co.uk

Customers in USA should contact:
Management Pocketbooks
2427 Bond Street, University Park, IL 60466
Telephone: 866 620 6944 Facsimile: 708 534 7803
E-mail: mp.orders@ware-pak.com
Web: www.managementpocketbooks.com